5 EASY WAYS TO BUILD YOUR YOUTUBE AUTHORITY

5 EASY WAYS TO BUILD YOUR YOUTUBE AUTHORITY

LUCAS KYLE

Bald and Bonkers Network Academy

CONTENTS

CHAPTER 1

Introduction

In the ever-evolving landscape of digital marketing, YouTube has emerged as a cornerstone for businesses aiming not just to survive but to thrive in the competitive online arena. Video promotion is no longer a mere supplementary tactic; it has become a central component in the arsenal of modern businesses seeking to resonate with their target audience effectively.

Beyond the visual appeal of images attached to blog posts, video content offers a multi-dimensional experience that captivates and retains the attention of viewers. The immersive nature of videos, combined with the storytelling potential they possess, sets them apart as a formidable tool for conveying complex messages in a digestible and engaging manner.

If the realm of YouTube marketing remains uncharted territory for your business, you might be pondering how to expand your digital footprint further. It's not merely about amassing views; it's about crafting a narrative that resonates with your audience, fosters trust, and positions your brand as a thought leader in your industry.

Building brand authority is a nuanced endeavor, and the creation of branded videos imparts a sense of authenticity and expertise that can't be replicated through traditional means. As consumers increasingly navigate the digital landscape, avoiding or ignoring traditional banner advertisements, the need for a more compelling and immersive form of online promotion becomes imperative.

Moreover, the prevalence of 'banner blindness' highlights the necessity of adopting alternative advertising methods. YouTube provides an avenue where your business can break through the clutter, offering valuable content that informs, entertains, and establishes a lasting connection with your audience.

The personal touch inherent in video content is a game-changer. By featuring yourself in your videos, you not only humanize your brand but also allow your audience to connect with the face and voice behind the business. This human element builds a sense of familiarity and trust, crucial elements in cultivating a dedicated and loyal customer base.

Now, let's delve into a more comprehensive exploration of the five strategic approaches that can be instrumental in enhancing your brand authority through the dynamic medium of YouTube. These strategies aim not only to increase your online visibility but also to position your business as a reliable source of information, a trendsetter, and an influential entity within your industry.

CHAPTER 2

Understand Your Views

Establishing your brand's authority on You-Tube is an intricate process that demands a keen understanding of your target audience and a strategic approach to content creation. The pivotal factor in this journey is crafting videos that not only align with your brand's message but also cater specifically to the desires and preferences of your viewers.

To embark on this endeavor, it's crucial to delve into a thorough comprehension of your audience. This involves more than just a surface-level understanding; it requires a deep dive into demographic details, encompassing factors such as age range, interests, and the genres of content they actively seek on YouTube. The aim is to create a profile of your ideal viewer, allowing you to tailor your content with precision.

Initiating a brainstorming session becomes the foundation of this process. It's an opportunity to meticulously consider the characteristics of your audience, their preferences, and the underlying motivations that drive them to engage with content similar to what your brand aspires to offer. By doing so, you set the stage for content that not only satisfies but surpasses the expectations of your target demographic.

An integral aspect of audience understanding involves conducting keyword searches related to your niche. This exercise unveils the current landscape of videos within your domain, shedding light on the type of content that resonates with viewers. Identifying videos with a high view rate becomes a key indicator, and delving into the corresponding channels provides valuable insights into subscriber numbers and patterns of audience engagement.

The meticulousness of your audience understanding becomes a linchpin in content creation. The more detailed and nuanced your insights, the better equipped you are to tailor your video content to meet the specific expectations of your audience. It's about crafting content that not only captures attention but also forges a lasting connection.

Defining your target audience is not merely a preliminary step; it's a foundational investment in the success of your YouTube channel. Before delving into the creative process of video production, taking the time to clearly outline the characteristics and preferences of your intended audience sets the groundwork for a strategic and impactful approach.

Building authority on YouTube necessitates providing content that not only attracts but also retains your target audience, prompting them to subscribe to your channel. This investment in understanding your audience pays dividends in the long run, as it positions your brand to curate content that resonates deeply with viewers, solidifying your presence in the competitive landscape of online video content. Remember, the journey to YouTube authority is not just about producing videos; it's about creating a community and forging meaningful connections through your content.

CHAPTER 3

Make Compelling Content

In the ever-evolving landscape of digital marketing, the adage "content is king" echoes through the corridors of various online platforms, from the written realms of blogging to the concise updates on Twitter, the visual allure of Facebook, and the dynamic world of YouTube. Yet, when it comes to the latter, the importance of content reigns supreme with even greater intensity. The pathway to cultivating a thriving YouTube presence and establishing authority unfolds through the creation of meticulously crafted, high-quality videos that possess the inherent potential to transcend their original platform and captivate audiences across diverse social media channels.

At the heart of this strategic endeavor lies the imperative need to comprehend your audience intimately. Crafting content that stands out, resonates, and is worthy of sharing necessitates a profound understanding of your viewers' preferences, interests, and the types of videos that elicit an enthusiastic response. This foundational knowledge serves as the compass guiding the trajectory of your content creation journey.

Delving into the question of what truly constitutes shareable content unveils a nuanced landscape. As seasoned content creators are well aware, the most shareable videos often fall into two distinctive categories: those that tickle the funny bone and those that tug at the heartstrings. While controversial content may momentarily capture attention, it lacks the enduring positive impact that heartwarming or humorous narratives tend to evoke.

A cautionary note emerges against the creation of mundane videos that feature a monotonous delivery against a backdrop of inanimate objects. An uninspiring presentation, devoid of excitement and humor, is unlikely to ignite interest, let alone inspire sharing. Such videos risk becoming lost in the vast expanse of digital content, impeding the growth of your followers and the establishment of authority on YouTube.

Instead, the strategic approach pivots toward the creation of a series of videos that not only showcase the merits of your product but also do so in an entertaining and engaging manner. The journey to discovering the video style that best suits your business inevitably involves experimentation. The iterative process is a voyage of exploration, with the final destination ideally being a style that seamlessly integrates both humor and entertainment.

The essence of the strategy lies in creating content that not only captures attention but also encourages viewers to share, thus amplifying its reach and impact. The dynamic nature of the journey toward YouTube authority demands an ongoing commitment to refining your approach, experimenting with various video styles, and adapting to the ever-evolving preferences of your audience.

In summary, the roadmap to YouTube authority unfolds as a dynamic and multifaceted expedition. A deep understanding of your audience, coupled with an unwavering commitment to high-quality, entertaining content, propels your brand toward increased visibility and authority within the intricate digital landscape. Through a strategic fusion of humor, entertainment, and continuous refinement, your brand can not only attract new followers but also solidify its position as a key player in the vibrant realm of online video content.

CHAPTER 4

Channel Branding

Building authority on YouTube is a multi-faceted process that extends beyond the creation of engaging content; it requires meticulous attention to branding and strategic optimization across various facets of your channel. An essential element in this endeavor is the seamless integration of your branding, ensuring a consistent visual identity not only on your company website but also across all social media platforms, including YouTube.

Customizing your YouTube channel to align with your business branding involves a comprehensive approach. Consistency in color schemes, tone, and style across online marketing platforms fosters a cohesive and recognizable image. By incorporating your company logo into your YouTube channel, either as the profile photo or within the channel banner, you establish a visual anchor that facilitates immediate brand recognition. This visual continuity plays a pivotal role in building a sense of familiarity and trust among viewers, forging a stronger connection with your content.

The permanence of your channel name on YouTube underscores the importance of selecting the right name during the content planning stage. This decision is integral, as it not only reflects your brand but also plays a crucial role in attracting the intended audience to your channel. The thoughtful selection of a channel name aligns with your broader marketing strategy, ensuring that your channel's identity resonates effectively.

Completing your YouTube channel profile with comprehensive details about your business and brand is a critical step. This comprehensive information not only enhances the credibility of your channel but also contributes to search engine optimization (SEO). Incorporating relevant keywords into your company description aids in securing a higher ranking on search engines, increasing the discoverability of your videos among your target audience.

Another powerful tool in enhancing the searchability of your videos is the strategic use of tags. Properly tagging your videos during each upload optimizes their visibility in search results. This meticulous approach to video optimization not only ensures that your content is of high quality but also makes it easily discoverable, increasing the likelihood of reaching your intended audience.

In essence, the meticulous alignment of your YouTube channel with your business branding, the strategic selection of your channel name, and the detailed completion of your channel profile are foundational steps in building authority on the platform. These elements, coupled with strategic keyword incorporation and effective video tagging, collectively contribute to a robust online presence. Through this holistic approach, your brand not only establishes authority on YouTube but also creates a unified and compelling identity that resonates with your target audience across diverse digital platforms, fostering long-term engagement and loyalty.

CHAPTER 5

Creating Different Kinds of Content

Building authority on YouTube necessitates a nuanced understanding of not only creating videos but strategically producing content that not only attracts views but also cultivates a growing subscriber base. In the dynamic realm of YouTube, the challenge is not merely to capture attention but to create content that resonates deeply with the target audience. While humor and entertainment are potent elements, exploring diverse video formats that have exhibited success on the platform is equally crucial.

For a discerning brand marketer, staying attuned

to the types of videos that enjoy popularity on YouTube is pivotal. Aligning your content strategy with prevailing trends can significantly amplify your channel's visibility and authority. The key lies in diversifying your video content around your product or service, ensuring a continuous stream of engaging material that keeps viewers interested and eager to return for more. Let's delve more comprehensively into some of the most effective types of content that can contribute to building authority on YouTube:

1. Product Reviews: In-depth and genuine product reviews offer valuable insights to potential customers, assisting them in making informed decisions. This type of content not only showcases your products but also establishes your brand as a trustworthy source of information.

2. How-to Videos: Step-by-step guides or tutorials that showcase the practical application of your product or service can position your brand as an authoritative figure, providing tangible value to your audience.

3. Video Blogs or Vlogs: Sharing the day-to-day operations, behind-the-scenes glimpses of your brand, or personal stories adds a human touch to your content. This fosters a sense of connection, allowing viewers to relate more intimately to your brand.

4. Comedy or Skit Videos: Infusing humor into your content makes it more shareable and enjoyable. Such videos create a positive association with your brand, making it memorable in the minds of your audience.

5. Educational Videos: Offering valuable insights or industry-specific knowledge positions your brand as an expert in the field. Educational content not only attracts viewers seeking to enhance their understanding but also establishes credibility.

6. Q&A Videos: Responding to questions from your audience fosters engagement and community-building. It creates a dialogue between your brand and your viewers, fostering a sense of connection.

7. Behind-the-Scenes Videos: Providing a transparent view into the inner workings of your business builds authenticity and trust. This type of content showcases the human side of your brand, establishing a more profound connection with your audience.

8. Webinars: Hosting webinars allows you to delve deeper into industry-related topics, showcasing your expertise and providing substantial value to your viewers. This format positions your brand as an authority in the field.

To effectively build authority on YouTube, it's imperative to venture out of your comfort zone and experiment with different content styles. While not every video format may seamlessly align with your business, early experimentation is vital to understanding what resonates best with your audience. Narrow down your selection to three or four content styles, and consistently rotate them to maintain audience interest. This dynamic approach ensures that your YouTube channel remains a dynamic and compelling source of content, attracting and retaining viewers while solidifying your brand's authority in the ever-evolving digital landscape.

CHAPTER 6

Marketing

The active promotion of your YouTube videos is a mission-critical component in the multifaceted journey of building authority on the platform. Beyond the creation of compelling content, effective promotion ensures that your videos reach your intended audience, thereby contributing significantly to your status as an authority in your niche. YouTube, recognizing the importance of cross-platform visibility, has streamlined the process with features such as auto-sharing, allowing content creators to seamlessly extend their reach to prominent social media platforms like Facebook and Twitter. This integration serves as a vital conduit for increasing the visibility of your content and fostering engagement with a broader audience.

Connecting your blog to your YouTube channel represents a strategic symbiosis that transcends the boundaries of individual platforms. This integration offers a seamless flow of content between your blog and YouTube channel, fostering a unified online presence. Whether you choose to directly post videos to your blog, embed them within written posts, or create a featured video for your homepage, these practices contribute to a cohesive brand identity and a dynamic online ecosystem. By providing multiple touchpoints for audience interaction, this approach enhances your authority by allowing viewers to engage with your content in various ways.

Expanding the network of links pointing towards your YouTube channel is a fundamental aspect of improving its discoverability in searches. By strategically placing links across your website, blog, and various social media accounts (including but not limited to Facebook, LinkedIn, Twitter, and Instagram), you not only facilitate cross-promotion but also send signals to search engines about the relevance and popularity of your content. This interconnected web is not only a promotional strategy but also a potent SEO tool, potentially resulting in higher rankings in both YouTube and Google searches.

Paid advertising emerges as a dynamic tool for accelerating visibility and subscriber growth. Platforms like Google Ads offer a range of flexible options, allowing you to showcase your ad before or alongside videos on YouTube watch pages. Crafting an engaging ad, defining a target audience, and setting a budget are pivotal steps in leveraging paid advertising effectively. Notably, the absence of a minimum ad spend on YouTube democratizes this advertising avenue, making it accessible to businesses of various sizes.

While there's no one-size-fits-all formula for creating the perfect video ad, numerous strategies can be employed. These may include storytelling, showcasing product features, or highlighting customer testimonials, depending on your brand and objectives. The dynamic nature of video advertising necessitates ongoing monitoring and analysis. This data-driven approach enables you to make timely adjustments to your advertising strategy, ensuring it evolves to deliver optimal results in alignment with your overarching goals.

In conclusion, the comprehensive promotion of your YouTube channel demands a strategic and multifaceted approach, combining auto-sharing features, blog integration, cross-platform linking, and potentially paid advertising. This holistic strategy not only amplifies the visibility of your content but also contributes to the establishment of authority within your niche. The interconnected nature of these promotional efforts not only attracts a wider audience but also ensures that your YouTube channel becomes a dynamic and influential force in the competitive landscape of online video content. Through these concerted and adaptive efforts, you not only capture attention but also solidify your position as a trusted and authoritative source within your industry.

CHAPTER 7

Final Thoughts

YouTube, traditionally renowned for hosting entertaining content, has undergone a transformative evolution, emerging as a pivotal tool for businesses to wield in their marketing arsenal. According to a recent report from the State of Inbound, the platform's increasing prominence is underscored by the fact that nearly half of all companies are gearing up to integrate YouTube into their marketing strategies within the next year. This surge in interest highlights YouTube's growing significance in the dynamic landscape of business marketing.

For small and medium-sized enterprises, recognizing and harnessing the potential of YouTube can prove to be a strategic move, offering a unique avenue to build brand awareness and establish authority within their respective industries. Implementing a comprehensive set of strategies becomes imperative for these businesses to not only create a YouTube channel that garners attention but also consistently draws in new audiences. This, in turn, contributes to the ongoing development of authority within their niches. If your business has not yet ventured into the realm of YouTube, the opportune moment to commence this journey is now.

Here, we delve into a more detailed exploration of the key strategies that businesses can adopt to establish a compelling and influential presence on YouTube:

1. Strategic Content Creation: Develop content with a deep understanding of your target audience, tailoring it to resonate with their preferences and align with your brand's message. Whether through educational videos, product demonstrations, or captivating storytelling, the content should not only capture attention but also provide tangible value to the viewers.

2. Consistent Branding: Ensure that your YouTube channel seamlessly aligns with your overall brand identity. Consistency in the use of colors, tone, and style across your videos and other marketing platforms reinforces brand recognition, creating a cohesive and memorable brand image.

3. Optimized Channel Setup: Leverage the features offered by YouTube to optimize your channel. This includes crafting a compelling channel description that succinctly communicates your brand identity, creating engaging channel art that visually captivates your audience, and designing well-thought-out video thumbnails for a professional and inviting channel appearance.

4. Active Community Engagement: Foster a sense of community by actively engaging with your audience through comments, likes, and shares. Responding to comments, soliciting feedback, and acknowledging viewer contributions not only build a community around your brand but also enhance loyalty and trust.

5. Strategic Promotion: Actively promote your YouTube content across various channels. This includes leveraging social media platforms for wider reach, embedding videos on your website to enhance visibility, and incorporating email marketing to keep your audience informed. Diversifying your promotional efforts broadens the reach of your content, attracting a wider and more diverse audience.

In summary, the trajectory of YouTube's evolution into a powerful marketing tool underscores its potential for businesses to thrive in the digital landscape. By implementing these strategies, businesses, irrespective of their size, can tap into the vast reach and engagement potential of YouTube to build brand authority, connect meaningfully with their audiences, and stay ahead in their respective industries. The time to embark on this YouTube journey is not just opportune but laden with boundless opportunities for growth and influence.

www.ingramcontent.com/pod-product-compliance
Lightning Source LLC
Chambersburg PA
CBHW071228140726
47996CB00004B/1523